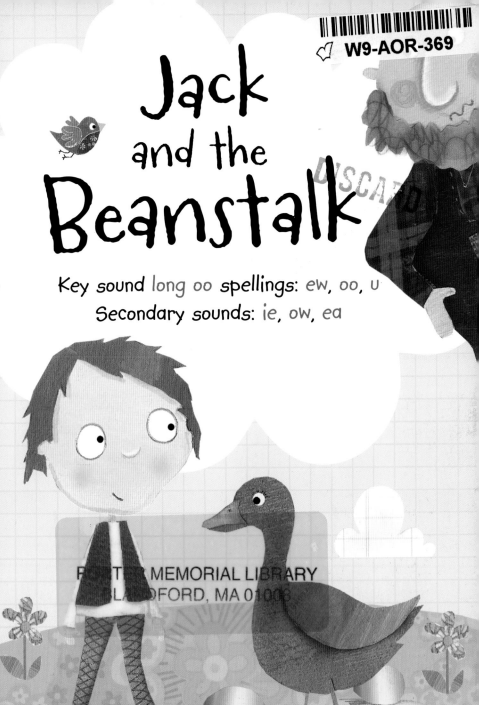

Jack
and the
Beanstalk

Key sound long oo spellings: ew, oo, u
Secondary sounds: ie, ow, ea

Written by Nick Page
Illustrated by Clare Fennell

Jack Pott and his mom
had a poor life, not much fun.
Food was scarce for those two
and their cow, called Little Moo.

Mom said, "Jack, you go now,
to the market, sell the cow.
I can't feed the both of you –
it's either you or Little Moo."

Fee-fi-foo-fum!
Jack Pott, what have you done?

A lady said, "Don't be blue.
I will buy that cow from you.
Can't pay cash – beyond my means –
instead, do use my magic beans."

Moo!

Back home, young Jack Pott
showed his mom the beans he got.
"You've been fooled!" his mother said.
"Throw them out and go to bed!"

Fee-fi-foo-fum!
Jack Pott, what have you done?

Next day, Jack awoke,
looked outside – was this a joke?
Something new now grew out there,
huge leaves rustled everywhere.

"Magic beans!" said Jack. "It's true!"
And now a beanstalk filled the view,
soared into the clouds so high,
climbing through the bright blue sky.

Fee-fi-foo-fum!
Jack Pott, what have you done?

9

Jack climbed up, and at the top,
a sight to make his eyes go "pop"!
A castle with huge rooms inside,
where everything was giant-sized.

Jack looked, and – behold! –
a blue goose laying eggs of gold.
"Rescue me!" honks the goose.
Jack says, "How could I refuse?"

Fee-fi-foo-fum!
Jack Pott, what have you done?

Boom!

Then – BOOM! – through the door,

a giant looms, begins to roar:

"Fee-fi-FOO-fum,

I smell the blood of an Englishman.

Be he alive, or be he dead,

I'll use his bones to grind my bread."

Jack says, "What a brute!"

And past the giant's boots he scoots.

Fee-fi-foo-fum!

Jack Pott, what have you done?

Jack runs off with his loot
and the giant in pursuit,
to the beanstalk with the goose,
while the giant screams abuse:

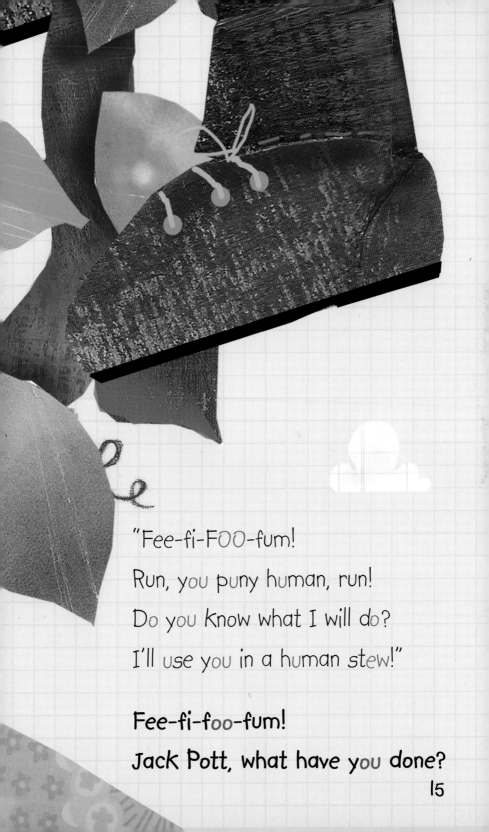

"Fee-fi-FOO-fum!
Run, you puny human, run!
Do you know what I will do?
I'll use you in a human stew!"

Fee-fi-foo-fum!
Jack Pott, what have you done?

15

16

Back home, Jack's mom says,
"You were grounded! Back to bed!"
"Quick!" says Jack. "No time to lose!
Cut the beanstalk! Hold this goose!"

Jack tells her all the facts.
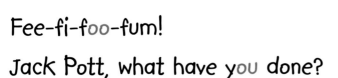
"Ooh!" she says. "Use this axe."
From above, a voice booms clear:
"I can see your house from here!"

Fee-fi-foo-fum!
Jack Pott, what have you done?

Ooh!

Jack Pott starts to chop,

then a voice comes from up top:

"Fee-fi-FOO-fum,

I smell the blood of an English mom!

In a goulash or fondue,

I'll have her boiled or barbecued!"

CHOP! CHOP! Cracks appear!

Goose shouts, "TIMBER! All stand clear!"

Fee-fi-foo-fum!

Jack Pott, what have you done?

Timber!

CREAK! CRACK! Suddenly,
the beanstalk falls like a toppled tree.
With a swooshing-whooshing sound,
the giant crashes to the ground.

BUMP! THUMP! Completely dead.

"He's been grounded," Jack's mom said.

Jack laughs, "What a hoot!"

Then he shows his mom the loot!

Fee-fi-foo-fum!

Jack Pott, what have you done?

"Ooh, Jack," said his mom.
"What a super-duper son!"
Jack knew what to do,
so he bought back Little Moo,
built a house for them all,
made the goose a swimming pool.
But Jack sometimes dreams . . .
"Maybe I should plant more beans?"

Fee-fi-foo-fum!

Jack Pott, what have you done?

Key sound

There are several different groups of letters that make the long oo sound. Practice them by following the different long oo coins to help Jack find the treasure.

true

brute

grew

chew

pool

fool

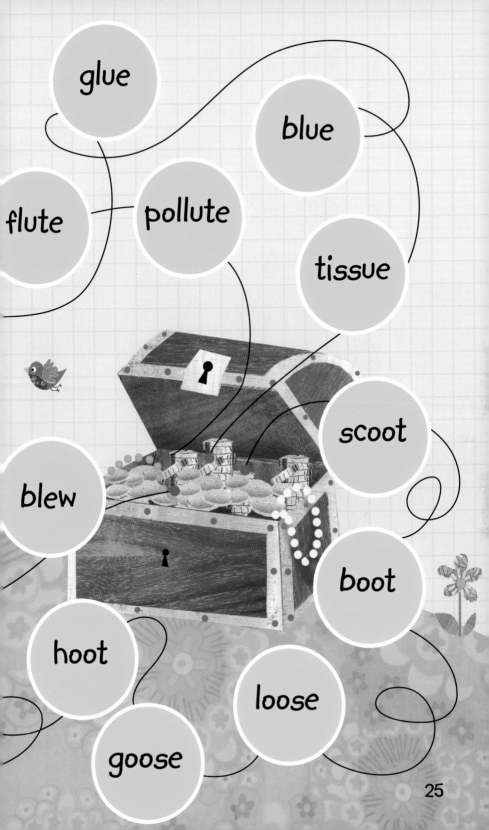

glue

blue

flute

pollute

tissue

scoot

blew

boot

hoot

loose

goose

25

Letters together

Look at these pairs of letters and say the sounds they make.

ie   **ow**   **ea**

Follow the words that contain **ie** to help the giant find the thief!

ie

chief   grief   waves

brief   lost

from   shriek

jumps   thief   right

26

Follow the words that contain ow to help Mom find Jack's cow.

the

other

ow

shower

owl

clown

flower

frown

lots

cow

down

Follow the words that contain ea to help Jack find the beanstalk.

ea

bean

leaf

suddenly

sea

please

other

beanstalk

gold

27

Rhyming words

Read the words in the flowers and point to other words that rhyme with them.

now	**cow**	leaves
how		blue

mean	**bean**	lean
gold		egg

pool	**brute**	bread
flute		chute